Managing
your
Money

Expert advice from:

Martina Collett
Careers and Employability Officer
South Thames College, London

Stephanie Fitzgerald
Head of Young People Programmes
The Money Charity
https://themoneycharity.org.uk

USBORNE

Managing your Money

JANE BINGHAM

AND HOLLY BATHIE

Designed by Vickie Robinson
and Stephanie Jeffries

Illustrated by Nancy Leschnikoff
and Freya Harrison

Edited by Felicity Brooks

USBORNE QUICKLINKS

The internet is a great source of financial information, but it's very important to know which sites you can trust.

We have selected some useful websites to supplement the information in this book and these are available at Usborne Quicklinks. Here you can find helpful tips on opening a bank account, saving money and making a budget, and learn more about topics such as student finance.

For links to all these sites, go to:

www.usborne.com/quicklinks

and enter the keywords 'managing your money'.

When using the internet, please follow the internet safety guidelines shown on the Usborne Quicklinks website. Children should be supervised whilst using the internet.

INTRODUCTION

This book is designed to help you take charge of your finances and make the most of your money. It's full of tips on how to earn money, how to be a smart spender and how to plan ahead, so you can spend your money on the things and people that really matter to you.

You'll learn how to make a budget, manage your expenses, and set aside money for giving and saving. You'll also look ahead to the kinds of financial choices you'll be making in the future.

The money habits you develop when you're young usually stay with you for life. So now's the time to start managing your money!

CONTENTS

HOW DO <u>YOU</u> MANAGE YOUR MONEY?

Are you confident that you're in charge of your finances, or do you feel you don't always make the most of your money?

Try the quick quiz on the next two pages to find out more about your money habits. Be as honest as you can, and don't worry about giving the 'right' answer. Learning to manage your money can take time and practice, but it's a skill that anyone can learn.

You could do the quiz again once you've finished the book, to see how much you've learned.

Quick Quiz

1. Do you always keep track of how much money you have?

A. No. I just spend my money, and stop when it runs out.

B. Sort of. I have a rough idea of how much money I have.

C. Yes. I keep a record of my money and my spending.

2. Do you ever find yourself running out of money?

A. Yes. I sometimes have to borrow from family or friends.

B. Almost never. I try to plan my spending.

C. Never. I always keep some money for emergencies.

3. Do you save up money for something special?

A. No. I'm hopeless at saving money.

B. Sometimes. But I often give up and spend the money instead.

C. Yes. I set aside a certain amount each week until I've reached my savings target.

4. You've been given a large gift of money. Do you . . .

A. Carry it with you in case you see something you want to buy.

B. Keep it in a safe place at home.

C. Put it in a bank account* where it can gain interest and grow.

   * You can read about bank accounts in Chapter 14.

5. You've spotted an amazing pair of shoes. Do you . . .

A. Buy them straightaway — you can't wait to make them yours.

B. Check if you can buy them at a cheaper price before you make your move.

C. Give yourself some thinking time. You might decide to spend your money on something else.

Answers

Mostly 'A' answers?

You've got a way to go before you're a money expert. But don't worry, you've just begun your journey.

Mostly 'B' answers?

You're usually sensible about money, but there are many useful skills you can discover.

Mostly 'C' answers?

You're already careful with money, but you can still learn from this book.

SO, WHAT IS MONEY?

When you think of money, what do you see?
Do you picture a pile of coins and notes? Or maybe
you think of something invisible, that can be sent
with a simple tap from a bankcard or smartphone?

Money has changed many times over the centuries,
and it's changing now faster than ever. So, how did
we get to where we are today? Here's a quick tour
through the history of money, from prehistoric times
to the present day ...

SWAPPING GOODS

For thousands of years, people didn't use money. Instead,
if they needed something (such as a camel), they found
something to swap for it (such as some goats).
This was known as bartering.

3 for 1!
It's a bargain!

SHELLS, BEANS AND BEADS

Around three thousand years ago,
some traders had a bright idea. Instead of
swapping actual things, they began using objects to
represent trading goods. Cowrie shells were used in
India and Africa. The Aztecs of Central Mexico
traded with cocoa beans, and some Native North
Americans used coloured beads, called 'wampum'.

METAL COINS

Metal coins were first used in Turkey around
the year 600BC. Later, the Ancient Greeks and
Romans each made their own set of coins, known
as a currency. Roman coins were stamped with the
head of the Emperor to show they were a currency
that could be trusted. Gradually, countries all over
the world developed their
own currencies.

PAPER MONEY

The first paper money was introduced in China in the 700s, but it was nearly a thousand years later that people in Europe began to print banknotes. In Europe, banknotes followed the creation of banks. A banknote is a promise from a bank to pay the amount printed on the note.

CHEQUES

In the 1700s, people started writing personal cheques. A cheque is a promise to transfer money from one bank account to another. Cheques were widely used until the end of the 20th century.

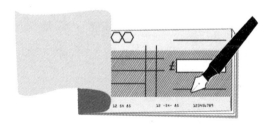

BANKCARDS

In the mid 1960s, a new way
of transferring money was
introduced. This was a plastic card
that could be recognized by a machine reader.
Bankcards are very useful for making payments,
and for taking money out of a bank account
using a cash machine.

ONLINE PAYMENT

By the 1990s, many people were paying for goods
online simply by typing the details of their bankcard
into a computer. This resulted in an automatic
transfer of money from buyer to seller. Online

payment led to the
rapid growth of online
selling companies.

CONTACTLESS PAYMENT

Around 2010, contactless payment was introduced. It allowed people to make an instant payment simply by holding a card or smartphone close to a machine reader. Contactless payments are not permitted for large sums of money. The upper limit in the UK is £30.

THINK BEFORE YOU TAP

Before you make a payment with a single tap, make sure you check the amount carefully. Even though you're not counting out coins and notes, it's still important to ask yourself: Do I REALLY have enough money to pay for this?

WHAT NEXT?

In the future, we may stop using cash altogether. Each time you make a payment, biometric scanners may recognize your face, your thumbprint or your voice, and transfer your money automatically.

The way we shop today is changing rapidly, with many people doing most of their spending online. In future, you may even use a shopping robot that's programmed to suggest what you should buy, based on your past spending choices.

What could we buy today?

BITCOIN — THE MONEY OF THE FUTURE?

In 2009, a new form of currency, known as 'bitcoin', was created. Bitcoin is a virtual currency (or cryptocurrency) that doesn't exist as coins or notes, but can be used on certain sites online. People pay for goods or services using bitcoins stored in an online wallet.

It's hard to predict if bitcoin will survive, but some people believe that we will all be using some form of cryptocurrency in the future.

THINKING ABOUT YOUR MONEY

A good way to start thinking about your money
is to ask yourself two simple questions:

- How much money do I have available to spend?
- How much money did I spend last week?

If you're struggling to answer these questions, you're
certainly not alone. But being vague about money can
make you feel uneasy. It can also lead to some
awkward situations when you discover
you've run out of cash.

I was sure I
had some money
somewhere.

Fortunately, it's possible to take some simple steps to keep on top of your spending, and the best place to start is with a money diary.

KEEPING A MONEY DIARY

Keeping a money diary will show you exactly how much money you have available to spend and how much you've paid out. Once you've gathered this useful information, you can start to plan ahead.

But first you need to choose the best way to keep your records ...

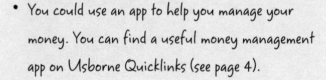

- You could use a notebook to jot down your spending.
- You could set up a money diary on a laptop, smartphone or tablet.
- You could use an app to help you manage your money. You can find a useful money management app on Usborne Quicklinks (see page 4).

MONEY IN AND MONEY OUT

Your money diary will show your money coming in (sometimes known as income or incomings) and your money going out (sometimes known as spending or outgoings).

To keep a record of money in, note down all the amounts you receive and where they come from. At the end of each week, add up your weekly total.

To keep a record of money out, note down each time you pay for something. Add up the total at the end of each day and keep a weekly total, too. That way, you can compare your spending from day to day and week to week.

KEEPING RECEIPTS

It isn't always easy to note down all your
spending, but if you keep receipts these will
show you exactly how much you've spent.
Try to get into the habit of adding up your
'money out' at the end of each day.
That way, you'll notice
straightaway if you've
spent too much.

WHERE DOES YOUR MONEY COME FROM?

Once you've set up a record of your money
coming in, you can start to think about where
it comes from.

REGULAR MONEY

You may receive weekly pocket money or a monthly
allowance. Or you may earn regular sums of money
in return for jobs. These are all amounts that you
can rely on when you're planning your spending.

> So, how much regular
> money do I have available
> to spend each week?

ABOUT ALLOWANCES

In any group of friends, there will always be some who have more spending money than others. But, whatever the size of your allowance, your challenge is to make your money work for YOU.

RANDOM AMOUNTS

Some of your 'money in' may be unexpected. Perhaps a relative has given you some money or you've won a prize? These are welcome extras, but they're not regular income so you can't include them when you plan ahead.

THINKING ABOUT YOUR MONEY IN

You may feel happy with the amount you have available to spend. Or you may decide you'd like to boost your income by earning extra money. There are ideas for earning money in Chapter 5.

WHAT DO YOU USE YOUR ALLOWANCE FOR?

Many teenagers are expected to use their allowance to pay for some essentials, such as food or clothes. This is very good practice for adult life, but it's important to be completely clear about the things your money is meant to cover.

For example:

- Will you be paying for lunches or only for snacks?
- Will you be buying everyday clothes or just a few fun extras?

It's a good idea to agree on some guidelines to help avoid any awkward misunderstandings.

HOW DO YOU SPEND YOUR MONEY?

Once you've recorded your 'money out' for a few weeks, you can start to think about your spending patterns. Here are some useful ways to look at what you've recorded:

• **What kind of things have I spent my money on?**

Try dividing your spending into different categories, such as food, clothes and presents. This will help you decide if you've got the balance right.

> Next month, **I'm** going to spend much less on clothes.

• **Are my purchases 'needs' or 'wants'?**

Learning to tell the difference between a need and a want is a vital money-managing skill. Find out more on page 29.

• Have I been charged too much?

Look through your records for high-priced items.

Then ask yourself, could I have got them cheaper?

(You can find tips on smart spending in Chapter 6.)

• Does my spending vary from week to week?

Try comparing your spending week by week.

You should be able to see at a glance if you've

been spending too much.

I must remember to look out for bargains.

Phew! I've been more careful with money this week.

NEEDS AND WANTS — CAN YOU TELL THE DIFFERENCE?

Next time you get ready to spend your money, stop yourself and ask: Is this a **need** or a **want**?

Needs are essentials that you can't manage without, such as shampoo to replace one that's run out.

Wants are luxuries that you don't really need, such as a second pair of trainers, in a different colour from the ones you already have.

It's fine to spend some money on wants, but first make sure you have enough to cover all your needs.

Quick Quiz

Take a look at the purchases below.
Can you decide which could be <u>wants</u> and which
could be <u>needs</u>? (Answers are on page 195.)

DEODORANT

sweets

MAGAZINE

CINEMA
TICKET

SANDWICHES

BANANA

perfume

lipstick

BUBBLEGUM

TOOTHPASTE

BUS
TICKET

SOCKS

MONEY IN AND MONEY OUT

Once you have a clear picture of your money 'in'
and 'out', you can compare the two. Add up the
weekly totals for your money in (income) and your
money out (spending) and put them side by side.
Then prepare to ask yourself some tough questions.
Looking at your money records, do you:

> a) Always make sure you have more money
> coming in than going out, so you
> have money to spare for an emergency.
> b) Sometimes struggle to keep a balance
> between money 'in' and 'out'.
> c) Sometimes find yourself spending
> more than you have coming in.

If you answered (a), you can relax, but if you
answered (b) or (c), you still have a way to go
before you become an expert money manager.

Money 'in' minus money 'out' = money left over

Sam's Money Diary

MONEY IN

Hmmm . . . I'd really like some more money to spend.

Week 1

Allowance	£10

Total = £10

Week 2

Allowance	£10
Garden jobs	£3

Total = £13

That's looking better. It's great earning extra money!

Week 3

Allowance	£10
Present from Gran	£5
Dog walking	£2

Total = £17

This week, I've got more income than I had last week, so I've decided to save some money.

MONEY OUT

Oh no – I've spent more than my allowance! (I owe Mum £1.50.)

Week 1

Muffin	£1.00	Ice cream	£2.00
Milkshake	£2.50	Popcorn	£1.00
Phone case	£5.00	Total = £11.50	

Week 2

Pay back Mum	£1.50	Cinema ticket	£6.00
Hot chocolate	£1.50	Crisps	50p
		Total = £9.50	

I've got more money to spend this week, but I've still been careful.

Week 3

Smoothie	£1.80		
Sandwich	£2.50	Flapjack	£1.20
Magazine	£4.50	Total = £10	

I'm saving up for headphones, so I've just spent my allowance this week and saved all the rest.

4. SETTING UP A BUDGET

Keeping a money diary will help you look back on your spending, but it's even more useful to plan your spending ahead. The best way to plan ahead is to set up a budget. This will show you how much money you have coming in and will also help you plan your spending.

INCOME, EXPENSES AND OTHER SPENDING

When you set up a weekly budget, the first thing you need to know is your **income** for the week.

Next, you need to note down all your **expenses**. These are payments that can't be avoided, such as bus tickets to get to school, college or work.

Once you've seen how much you need to spend on expenses, you can work out how much money you have left for **other spending.**

CREATING A BUDGET

One of the best ways to set up a budget is to create a simple spreadsheet on your computer, tablet or smartphone. Spreadsheets have columns which you can use to show your income, your expenses, and your other spending. Using a simple spreadsheet will let you compare totals so you can see at a glance if you have enough income to cover your expenses, and how much money you have left for other spending.

BUDGETING HELP

Go to Usborne Quicklinks (see page 4) to download a budget spreadsheet and to find a link to a budget-building app.

MAKING A WEEKLY BUDGET

To make a simple weekly budget, you need two columns: one for **income** (money coming in) and one for **expenses** (money you need to set aside to spend on essentials).

When you subtract your expenses from your income, you can see how much money you have left, and plan your spending for the week ahead.

Take a look at Callum's weekly budget, showing his income and his expenses.

Income		Expenses	
Allowance	£15.00	2 x lunches	£10.00
Dog walking	£5.00	Bus tickets	£3.00
Total	**£20.00**	**Total**	**£13.00**

I need to subtract my expenses from my income to see what I have left to spend.

£20
- £13
= £7

PLANNING YOUR SPENDING

Once you've calculated your spending money for the week, you can add a section to your budget for 'other spending'. Make sure this total doesn't add up to more than you have left to spend.

Income		Expenses		Other spending	
Allowance	£15.00	2 x lunches	£10.00	Magazine	£2.50
Dog walking	£5.00	Bus tickets	£3.00	Snacks & drinks	£4.00
Total	£20.00	Total	£13.00	Total	£6.50

I need to stay inside my spending limit of £7.00, so I'm planning to spend £6.50 this week.

MONEY LEFT OVER

If you have money left over at the end of the week, you could add it to your income for the following week, or you could put it in your savings fund.

See Chapter 13 for more on saving.

EXPANDING YOUR BUDGET

Budgets can be simple, like the one shown in this chapter, or they can have many extra columns. For example, you could add a column for your savings to your weekly budget.

WHO NEEDS A BUDGET?

Everyone really. Companies and governments set up detailed budgets to plan how they'll spend their money and to make sure they don't overspend. Some families also use budgets to plan their household spending. You can make a budget for a week, a month, a year or longer.

5. EARNING MONEY

There are many ways to earn money of your own. Take a look at the ideas on the next few pages and think about which ones could work for you.

PART-TIME JOBS

If you're 14 or older, you may be able to find some part-time work in a local shop, business or café.

As well as providing regular money, a part-time job will give you valuable experience of the world of work and will equip you with some useful skills.

BEFORE YOU START A PART-TIME JOB . . .

- Check with your parents or guardians that they are happy for you to take on a regular job.
- Make sure you can work the hours that have been agreed. (If you have exams coming up, talk to your employer.)
- Ask for a letter or contract from your employer, stating your working hours, pay and conditions of work. That way, you'll be prepared, just in case there's a problem.

JOBS AT HOME

Some parents are happy to pay for jobs around the home. Why not try suggesting some of the jobs on this page? (Don't be surprised if you're expected to tidy your room for nothing, though.)

Dusting

WASHING THE CAR

CLEARING OUT CUPBOARDS

VACUUMING

RAKING UP LEAVES

MOWING THE LAWN

WATERING PLANTS

JOBS FOR FRIENDS AND NEIGHBOURS

Once you're confident that you have some useful
skills, you could offer to work for neighbours and
friends. Maybe you could mow your neighbours'
lawn or put out their rubbish bins? Or perhaps
you could feed their cat or water
their plants while they're
on holiday?

SAFETY FIRST

When you're working for
neighbours, stick to people you
know. Don't go into strangers' houses and don't
give out any contact details without checking
first with your parents or guardians.

WORKING WITH ANIMALS

If you're good with animals, you
could help friends and neighbours by . . .

• Pet-sitting

This usually involves feeding a pet at regular times
and making sure it's happy and healthy.

• Cleaning out cages or hutches

Some pet owners may be more than happy to hand
over this job. And if you like horses, you may be able
to earn regular money by helping out at a stables.

• Dog walking

This is a good job if you like walking,
but you'll need to be confident that
you can keep the dogs under control.

HELPING WITH CHILDREN

The recommended age for baby-sitting is 16, but you can be a parents' helper before you reach that age. If you know some parents who work from home, you could offer to help look after their children after school — feeding them, reading to them and keeping them entertained.

IT SUPPORT

Your IT skills could come in very useful if any of your friends or family need help getting to grips with technology. Perhaps you could help them find their way around a smartphone or tablet, or help them to set up their computer?

PARTY ENTERTAINMENT

Are you good at juggling, magic tricks or face-painting? If so, you could help with children's parties.

When you're entertaining young children, it can be easier to work with someone else. You could get together with a friend to present a magic display or a puppet show, but you'll need to put in some practice first.

SHARING JOBS

When you share a job with friends, you have to share the money you make as well. Make sure you charge enough to make the job worthwhile for everyone. You can find advice on charging for your work on pages 48 to 51.

MAKING THINGS

Do you like designing and making things? And can you use your skills to make attractive items to sell? Here are just a few ideas to help you get started...

- You could sew, knit or crochet hats, clothes or toys.
- You could produce calendars and cards.
- You could create ornaments and jewellery.
- You could make an attractive bird feeder.

You'll find instructions for making things on Usborne Quicklinks (see page 4).

MAKING A PROFIT

When you decide on a price for something you've made, it's important to be sure that you can make a profit. A profit is the difference between the price of an item and the costs involved in making it.

Think about the money you've had to pay out. Maybe you've bought beads for making jewellery? Or perhaps you've paid to print posters to advertise your sale? If you want to make a profit, your price will need to cover these costs.

We've worked out what to charge for our cards so we can make a profit.

You can see how we've calculated our price on pages 50 to 51.

YOUR TIME MATTERS TOO

If you were making a hand-made present for your granny, she would really appreciate the time it took you to make her gift. But if you were earning money from selling hand-made goods, it would be important to add the cost of your time to what you charge. For example, if you were knitting hats, you would need to include a cost for your time as well as the cost of the wool.

BE REALISTIC

Of course, you want to make a profit on the things you're selling, but when you're setting your prices, you'll need to be realistic too. Look at the prices of similar things. You probably won't be able to charge much more.

AMIT AND AMY'S PLAN TO MAKE A PROFIT

This is the plan we made to sell our cards . . .

First, we decided how many
cards we wanted to make.

Let's make **100** cards.

Then we thought about what materials we would
need and how much they would cost.

Materials	Cost	Quantity	Totals
card	60p per sheet	10 sheets	£6.00
tissue paper	£5 per packet	2 packets	£10.00
glue stick	£1 per stick	2 sticks	£2.00

Total cost = £18.00

Next, we divided this total by the number of cards to find
the materials cost of one card.

£18.00 divided by 100 = **18p**

Each card will cost us
18p in materials.

But we still needed to add in the cost of our time . . .

First, we calculated the labour cost of each card.

> Let's say the labour cost of us both making cards is £10 an hour.

> Between us, it will take an hour to make 20 cards, so we need to divide £10 by 20.

£10 ÷ 20 = 50p

> The labour cost is 50p for each card.

Then we added the materials cost to the labour cost to find the cost of making one card.

18p + 50p = 68p

> Each card costs us 68p to make.

Using this information, we decided on a price per card that would cover all our costs AND make a profit.

> What would our profit be if we charged £1.50 a card?

£1.50 (price per card) minus 68p = 82p

> We're making a profit of 82p on each card. So, how much would we make if we sold all 100 cards?

£0.82 (profit per card) x 100 = £82.00

> £82 is a good profit!

Quick Quiz

Can you work out how to make a profit?

(Answers are on page 195.)

a) If the cost of materials to make 12 hand puppets is
£30, what is the cost of materials for each puppet?

Materials cost per puppet = _____

b) If you charge £8 per hour for your labour (work)
and you make 4 puppets an hour, how much will it cost
you to make each puppet?

Labour cost per puppet = _____

c) Can you calculate the total cost of making each
puppet? (Total cost = materials cost + labour cost)

Total cost per puppet = _____

d) How much should you charge for each puppet
if you want to make a profit of £1.50 per puppet?

Price per puppet = _____

SMART SPENDING

6

How do some people manage to make their money go so far, while others keep running out of funds? This chapter offers advice on how to be a smart spender and save money on:

- food and drink
- clothes and shoes
- beauty and grooming products

It also shows you how to get to grips with discounts, price cuts and special offers.

But, first, take a look at the spending tips on the next page.

1. SLOW DOWN

Before you spend any money, stop and ask yourself:
Do I really need this? Or do I just want it?

2. PLAN AHEAD

Think about what you need in advance and try to
avoid impulse buys. It's easy to make bad choices
when you're feeling rushed.

3. PLAY IT SAFE

Always keep your receipt and check that you can
return your purchase if you need to. (You can read
about returns and refunds in Chapter 9.)

FOOD AND DRINK

Buying food and drink is one of the biggest expenses that most teenagers face. Of course, it's important to eat plenty of healthy food, but there are some simple ways to cut down on your spending and still end up with healthy, tasty food.

Next time you go shopping for food, try these money-saving tips:

• **Compare prices for similar products.**
Take a few minutes to check the prices for different brands. You may be surprised to see how much they vary.

• **Look out for supermarket own-brand products.**
Own-brand products can be just as good as the well-known brands, but they often cost less.

- Aim to shop at the end of the day.

  You'll usually find some items, such as bread from the bakery, have been reduced for a quick sale.

- Don't be fooled by packaging.

  A packet of apple slices may look appealing, but if you buy a whole apple, it will taste fresher and it will cost less.

- If there's something you eat a lot, buy it in bulk.

  A multipack of cereal bars is cheaper than the same number of individual bars and it should keep you going for several days.

BUY IN TIME

You can find bargains in the reduced section of most supermarkets, but if you're buying meat, fish or dairy products, check their sell-by dates and make sure you use them straightaway.

WHAT ABOUT SPECIAL OFFERS?

Special offers and discounts can be good money savers, but don't get drawn into buying something you don't need. Before you go for that tempting three-for-two offer, remember to ask yourself:

Why am I buying more than I really need?

STICK TO YOUR LIST

Do you sometimes arrive at the checkout with all sorts of things you don't really need? If you write a shopping list and stick to it, it will help you avoid expensive impulse buys.

CALCULATING DISCOUNTS

Here is a quick way to calculate discounts that are shown as percentages. If you first work out 10% (ten percent) of the original price, you can use this amount to calculate other percentages.

You can calculate 10% of the original price by dividing the price by 10.

The discounted price is
£15 minus £1.50 discount = £13.50.

Now you know that 10% of the original price is £1.50, you can use this figure to work out other discounts.

A discount of 20% is 10% x 2.

The discounted price is

£15 minus £3.00 discount = £12.00.

£1.50
x 2
= £3.00
discount

A discount of 40% is 10% x 4

The discounted price is

£15 minus £6.00 discount = £9.00.

£1.50
x 4
= £6.00
discount

DISCOUNTS AT A GLANCE

Many people find it easier to think in fractions, such as halves and quarters, rather than percentages. Here's a quick guide to some common discounts:

50% off = 1/2 price

33% off = 1/3 (a third) off

25% off = 1/4 (a quarter) off

75% off = 3/4 (three quarters) off

WHAT'S THE BEST VALUE?

It can be hard to tell if you're getting value for money when food comes in so many different packages. But luckily, there is a way to compare prices.

How can I tell which one is the best value for money?

Shops selling food and drink are required by law to show the unit price of the goods on sale. This is the cost of goods per item or per measure (for example, per kilogram or per litre).

LOOK FOR THE UNIT PRICE

Look for the unit price at the bottom of the price label. This will allow you to compare the cost of items, even when they're packaged in very different ways.

Orange juice (1 litre)

£1.00

£1.00/litre

Orange juice (2 litres)

£1.66

83p/litre

This is the best value.

Bag of oranges (5 pack)

£1.25

£0.25/each

Oranges (loose)

35p

£0.35/each

It's cheaper to buy the bag of oranges rather than five loose oranges.

BUYING CLOTHES AND SHOES

Shopping for clothes and shoes can be a lot of fun,
but it's all too easy to make expensive mistakes.
Next time you're tempted to pay out lots of money,
ask yourself these questions:

• Does it really fit ?

Is it too big or too small? Does it feel uncomfortable?

• When will I wear it?

Do you really want to spend a lot of money on
something you'll only wear a few times?

• Is it hard to keep clean?

Clothes that are 'dry clean only' work
but to be very expensive in the long run.

• Do I have something almost the same at home?

Is it a want or a need? (Turn back to page 29
to remind yourself about wants and needs.)

If you still feel happy with your choice,
it's time for the next big question.

Am I paying too much?

This is when you need to do some checking . . .

If you're out shopping, check out other shops
to see if you can find something cheaper. You can
usually ask for an item to be reserved for a short
time, while you decide if you really want to buy it.
You can also check online to see if you can buy the
same item at a cheaper price.

If you're shopping online, search other sites for
special offers or sales.

Once you've done your research, you may choose
to go ahead — confident that you've got a good deal.
Or you may decide to hold back for a while. This will
give you time to look around some more, or to wait
for a sale when you can find some bargains.

PRELOVED CLOTHES

You can find some amazing bargains in second-hand shops or on selling sites online. Often, clothes and shoes that have never even been worn are sold at a fraction of their original cost.

Charity shops are excellent places to look for interesting clothes. And you'll be contributing to a good cause, as well as saving money.

Some people create a distinctive style by putting together vintage items from charity shops. Even if you don't buy a whole outfit, you might like to buy a few retro items.

TOILETRIES AND BEAUTY PRODUCTS

Of course you want to look — and smell — your best, but before you blow your cash on the latest 'magic formula', take a look at the advice below.

- Try before you buy. Ask for a tester sample to try, and only buy products that you're sure are right for you.

- Don't let glamorous adverts push you into buying top-price items. Check out beauty and grooming blogs for lower-cost options.

- Test out creams and fragrances on your skin and wait a while before you hand over your money. You may have an allergic reaction to some products.

- Hold a party with your friends, and swap the products that don't work for you.

IT'S OK TO MAKE MISTAKES

Don't get too demoralized if you feel you've wasted your money. Everyone makes shopping mistakes sometimes. Think of them as useful experiences in your progress to becoming a smart spender.

Quick Quiz

Can you spot a bargain, or do you get confused by special offers? Take a look at these offers and decide which is the best deal in each pair. (Answers are on page 195.)

a) **2 FOR 1** OR b) **SECOND ITEM 1/2 PRICE**

c) **2/3 ORIGINAL PRICE** OR d) **20% off**

e) *half price* OR f) **60% OFF**

Can you work out the new, discounted, price of the clothes below?

SHORTS £20 NOW 25% OFF

T-SHIRT £12 NOW 1/3 OFF

----------------------   ----------------------

7

BUYING AND SELLING ONLINE

Online shopping is a good way to compare prices, find bargains and save yourself money, but it can come with risks. So, how can you protect yourself online and enjoy shopping in safety?

BE A SAFE SHOPPER

Make sure your parents know about what you are planning to buy online. If you follow the guidelines below, they will also help to keep you protected.

- Always use a secure internet connection for your online shopping so your financial details can't be stolen.

- Avoid public Wi-Fi sites, such as in cafés or shopping centres, where other users could access your information.

- Check that the seller's website is secure. Look out for a padlock symbol in the address bar next to the website address. If you click on this symbol and a warning comes up, leave the site.

- Take a careful look at the seller's returns policy. (You can find out more about returns in Chapter 9.) Sites with no information on returns should be avoided.

- Choose strong passwords for your online accounts, using a combination of upper and lower case letters and numbers.

- If you're asked if you want to 'save' your card details, always play safe and tick 'no'.

- And finally — be suspicious! If a deal seems too good to be true, it probably is.

ONLINE AUCTIONS — THINK BEFORE YOU BID

Online auctions can be exciting, but you need to be careful
not to get carried away. You can end up spending much
more than you'd planned and then there's no going back.
If your bid is successful, you will be committed to buying
an item and you might not have the right to return it.

ONLINE SELLING

Online selling can be a good way to clear your clutter and make money, but it's very important to stick to some basic safety rules.

- Never contact buyers or sellers yourself. Ask a parent or guardian to do it for you.
- Make sure you don't appear in any photos of items for sale.
- Always follow the safety guidelines provided by selling sites.

You could also think about getting together with friends or family members to sell your unwanted clothes, books and games.

8

PHONES, GAMES AND APPS

Your phone can be a major money guzzler. Charges can mount up fast, and phones can be damaged, lost or even stolen. Here are some ways to help cut your costs and keep your phone safe.

BUYING A PHONE

There will always be pressure to have the latest model, but buying something less flashy could be a smarter move. If you go for a less expensive phone:

- You won't feel so upset if you damage or lose it.
- It won't cost a fortune to replace.
- You'll have more money to spend on other things.

I'm so retro, I'm back in fashion.

LOOKING AFTER YOUR PHONE

- Always keep your phone in a safe place.
- Invest in a sturdy cover to protect it from knocks and drops.
- Make sure your phone is password protected — and don't choose a password that's easy to guess.
- NEVER keep important financial information, such as your bank PIN, on your phone.
- Consider insuring your phone, so you can cover the cost of replacing it. (Phones can usually be covered by a family's home contents insurance, see page 172.)

AND IF IT GOES MISSING . . .

- Let your parents or guardians know straightaway.
- Contact your network provider and report it missing.

LOOKING AT CONTRACTS

You need to be 18 to have your own mobile phone contract, but if you are younger it's still useful to know the choices available, to help your family choose the right one for you.

Phone contracts offer a fixed allowance of texts and minutes for calls, in return for a monthly charge known as a tariff. Smartphone contracts will also include an allowance for data (use of the internet). So long as you stay inside your tariff, you can predict how much you'll be paying each month. But as soon as you go over your allowance, you will find yourself facing extra charges (unless you have a capped contract, see opposite page).

There are many different tariffs on offer, so you'll need to choose one that fits the way you use your phone. It's also a good idea to choose a flexible contract that allows you to change to a different tariff if you realize it's better suited to your needs.

CHECK YOUR PHONE USE

Get into the habit of checking to see if you've stayed inside your tariff. If you find you're being charged for extra data use, think about switching to a contract with a more generous data allowance.

I check my usage at the end of each week.

CAPPED CONTRACTS

Some phone contracts come with an automatic cap. This means that once you've used up your month's allowance, calls, texts or data access are blocked until the end of the month. Many families choose to have a capped contract, so the bill-payer is never faced with unexpected charges.

SIM ONLY CONTRACTS

Many phone contracts include the price of a phone, but with a SIM only contract you supply your own phone. The phone service company simply provides the SIM card to go inside your handset and charges you for the use of your phone.

As well as being cheaper than most standard contracts, SIM only deals allow you to change your tariff more easily. Some deals even permit you to adjust your tariff month by month.

PAY AS YOU GO

One sure-fire way to make sure you don't overspend is to go for a prepaid 'pay as you go' (PAYG) phone deal. This is not a contract, so you can have a PAYG phone at any age.

Anyone can use pay as you go!

With a PAYG deal, you use your own phone. You make your payment to the phone service company in advance, and your phone stops working as soon as you've used up your money. A PAYG deal allows you to pay if and when you can afford it, and you can even decide not to use your phone for a while.

CUT YOUR PHONE COSTS

The most common reason for exceeding your tariff is excess data use. Here are some ways to cut down on data use on your smartphone.

- Connect to a local Wi-Fi source whenever you can, and turn off data roaming.
- Switch off any apps and games you're not using.
- Beware of data gobblers, such as films, live-streamed videos and TV programmes.

GAMING

If you're into gaming, you can find yourself paying out serious money. As well as the cost of the games, there are tempting ads for bigger and better consoles, keyboards, controllers and headsets.

You can make a big difference to your costs if you decide NOT to buy everything new. You could set up a swap group with your friends, or look online for pre-owned games and sell your own unwanted games. That way, you'll be spending less and having more gaming fun.

WATCH OUT FOR HIDDEN COSTS

Many games apps that are free to download are designed to encourage you to pay out money. Just as the game is getting exciting, a message will flash up on the screen, asking if you want to access more levels, win back lives or buy new objects. If you're not very careful, you can find yourself pressing the 'buy now' button, without even stopping to think about the cost. Turn over to find out more about in-app payments.

 ## IN-APP PURCHASE WARNING

Whenever customers register with an app store, they are asked for details of their bankcard. Each time the customer presses 'buy' inside an app, the payment is charged automatically to their card. This can result in some serious expense, and there are stories of kids spending thousands of pounds on their parents' bankcards without even realizing they've paid out real money.

Fortunately, there's a way to avoid unexpected expense on in-app payments. If you register a prepaid card with a set amount of money, you will never go beyond your payment limit. (See page 118 for more about prepaid cards.)

FREE TRIAL ALERT

Some apps that are free to download are actually subscriptions that can end up costing you money every month.

Watch out for apps with a free trial period. This usually lasts a month, and after that date you can find yourself facing monthly charges.

Remember to note the date when the free trial ends so you can cancel your subscription. Otherwise, payments will be taken automatically from your bankcard. And once you've started paying monthly subscription fees, you may face a cancellation fee when you try to stop them.

Give me more money NOW!

RETURNS AND REFUNDS (PLAYING SAFE)

9

Even experienced shoppers sometimes make mistakes, especially when they're buying things online. You can end up with something that's faulty or damaged, the wrong size or colour, or even completely different from what you'd expected. Luckily, this needn't mean you've wasted your money. As long as you follow the rules explained in this chapter, you will usually be able to return your purchase and get your money back.

I was expecting a smaller hat!

CHECK BEFORE YOU BUY

Before you hand over your money, you need to make sure you won't be stuck with something you can't return.

- If you're in a shop, ask a sales assistant about their refund policy before you make your payment. Or you can look for a sign near the till.
- If you're shopping online, find the section headed 'Returns' and read it through carefully before confirming your order.
- Some items are almost always non-returnable, such as underwear and earrings.

SALE WARNING

When shops hold sales to clear out their old stock, there are special rules for returning sale items. Often, there's only a short time allowed for returning a purchase, and some sale items can't be returned at all.

REMEMBER TO KEEP YOUR RECEIPT

If you want to return an item, you'll need to show your receipt as proof of purchase. Some shops provide e-receipts, but many still use paper receipts. Shops usually have a time limit for returns, such as 14 or 28 days, so try to get into the habit of keeping your paper receipts in a special place, such as a shoebox, so you know exactly where to find them.

If you've lost your receipt, the seller may still take back the unwanted item, but instead of a refund you may be given a credit voucher to spend in their shop.

I wish I'd kept my receipt somewhere safe.

REFUNDS AND CREDIT VOUCHERS

A refund is a repayment of the exact sum that you paid. You are entitled to a refund if an item is faulty and you have proof of purchase, if you've followed the seller's returns policy (see page 86).

If you're returning something simply because you've changed your mind, you may be offered a credit voucher. Credit vouchers are sometimes known as credit notes or store credits, and they can be a plastic card or a printed slip. A credit voucher allows you to buy goods up to the value of the item you've returned. Most credit vouchers can only be used in the shop (or chain of shops) where you made your purchase and they often have a time limit.

LOOK AFTER YOUR CREDIT VOUCHER

- Make sure you use it before the time limit or you'll end up losing all the money you spent.
- Keep it in a safe place. There's no way to claim your money back if you've lost your voucher.

RETURNING YOUR PURCHASES

Sellers can insist on certain terms before they agree to take back a purchase and refund your money.

• Always check the time limit for returning goods.
If you return your purchase after the time limit, the seller has the right to refuse a refund.

• Check any other terms and conditions.
Often these conditions state that an item must be returned in exactly the same condition as it left the seller, with the original packaging, tags or labels. This means clothes or shoes mustn't show any signs of wear. If you wear your new shoes outside — even for just a few minutes — the soles will get dirty and you won't be allowed a refund.

- Items bought online and delivered to your home need to be returned in the same packaging.

Even if you can't wait to see inside your package, open it carefully in case you need to send it back.

LOOKING AT A RECEIPT

This is the date of purchase. It proves you're returning your goods in the time allowed.

```
      GIFTS GALORE
       01.07.2019

STAR CANDLE   4.50
              -----
TOTAL         4.50
VISA DEBIT
Verified by PIN
```

This shows exactly how much you paid so you can be refunded the right amount.

This indicates that you paid by bankcard, so any money refunded will be put back into your bank account. If you originally paid in cash, you will be given a cash refund.

10. HAVING FUN

Having fun with friends can end up being very expensive. So, how do you have a good time without spending a fortune?

What to do...

IN OR OUT?

You don't always have to go out to have a good time. Why not try planning some 'time in' with your friends? That way, you'll save money, and your 'time out' will feel more special. Look at the page opposite for some ideas.

SETTING LIMITS

Sometimes you can end up spending a lot more on going out than you'd planned. But if you get together with friends to plan your outing, you can decide on a spending limit in advance.

Once you know exactly how much you'll be spending, you can relax and enjoy yourself, knowing that your costs won't get out of hand.

FIVE MONEY-SAVING IDEAS FOR FUN TIMES IN

1. Have a movie night at home. Make some popcorn, dim the lights and settle down to enjoy a film.

2. Try living-room karaoke. Clear a space for a stage, and sing along to your favourite songs.

3. Organize a craft session and share your skills. You could perhaps turn what you make into money-saving gifts.

4. Hold a board games afternoon. (You can buy games cheaply in second-hand shops), roll the dice and start playing.

5. Hold a dance competition. Download some dancing tracks and try out some moves.

CUTTING COSTS

Often, the biggest expense when you're going out is the money you spend on food and drink. With just a little planning, you can cut down on these costs.

I fill up my water bottle as I go. That way, I save money and help the environment.

I take home-made food to share with my friends.

I make my own smoothies. They save me lots of money!

I take my own hot drink rather than paying **coffee shop** prices.

We take our own food and drinks to the cinema. Otherwise, our snacks can end up costing more than the film!

(Most cinemas allow you to bring your own cold snacks and soft drinks.)

MEAL DEALS

If you decide you want to eat out, it pays to shop around for special deals. Look out for:

- Restaurants that offer an early evening rate.
- Vouchers from cafés and restaurants offering special deals. (But check the conditions — some deals are not as good as they first seem.)
- Apps to help you track down the best value meals near you.

(Remember to check that the special offer or discount has been correctly applied to your bill.)

FIVE MONEY-SAVING IDEAS

FOR FUN TIMES OUT

1. Organize a ball game in the park.
2. Go on a bike ride with your friends.
3. Visit a free museum or gallery.
4. Search online for free events near you.
5. Look out for family vouchers for

   special attractions.

GIVING PRESENTS

11

One of the most satisfying ways to use your money is to spend it on others. There's nothing like the feeling of giving a treat to someone you care about. So, how can you make the most of your money and give the kind of presents that show you care?

IT'S THE THOUGHT THAT COUNTS

You don't need to spend a fortune to make someone's day. Instead, you can use your time and talents to create something that's unique. Here are some ideas for gifts that will make the most of your money:

- Create a picture frame for a special photo.
- Decorate a jar and fill it with home-made biscuits.
- Paint a flowerpot and plant some herbs in it.
- Make a calendar using your own photos.
- Bake and decorate a cake.

BIRTHDAY PROMISES

Do you sometimes have trouble thinking of the perfect present? Perhaps you could promise a treat instead? Think of something special that the person you're treating would really enjoy. Then write out your promise in a card.

I promise to . . .

PUT ON A
SHOW FOR
YOU

BRING YOU
BREAKFAST
IN BED

Clean the house

WRITE YOU
A STORY

BUDGETING FOR PRESENTS

Are there times when you'd like to spend money on presents, but you find that you just don't have enough to spare? If so, you could look at building up a gift fund.

Once you've made a weekly budget for yourself, you can add a column for gifts. You could plan to save a regular amount each week, and, in the weeks before a busy present-buying time, you could increase the amount you set aside for gifts.

I usually set aside £2 a week for gifts.

Next month, I need to buy lots of presents, so I'm saving £5 a week.

12

GIVING TO CHARITY

When you give money to charity, you help make a difference — to other people's lives, to the environment or to wildlife. It's good to know you're helping in some way and you don't have to be rich to be a charity champion:

- You can budget to make a donation to a cause you support.
- You can help some charities through your shopping choices.
- You can use your time and energy to raise money for a special cause.

I make cards and sell them for charity.

I buy Fairtrade products whenever I can.

RAISING MONEY

Raising money for charity is very rewarding — and it can be good fun too. Why not get together with friends and plan what you can do to raise some funds?

FIVE IDEAS

FOR RAISING MONEY

1. Organize a car-washing team.

2. Put on a song and dance show.

3. Plan a sponsored run, swim, or sing.

4. Hold a bake sale.

5. Set up a face-painting stall.

GAINING SKILLS

When you raise money for charity, you're not just supporting an important cause. You're also gaining some valuable money-managing skills that will help you in your adult life.

FINDING SPONSORS

A good way to boost your charity funds is to find some sponsors. You could try approaching local shops or businesses and asking them if they'd like to help.

- They may be willing to pay for some of your costs.
- They may donate food, equipment or prizes.
- They may offer to match the money you raise.

In return for your sponsors' help, you can display their names as supporters of your event. Don't forget to include all the important information on a poster or flyer.

Date, time and place

Name of event

Name of charity

Name of sponsor

14 MAY, 4PM, AT THE FOOTBALL CLUB

CHARITY DOG SHOW

All proceeds go to the
Puppy Protection League

LOTS OF EXCITING PRIZES!

SPONSORED BY
JUICY BONES

13. STARTING TO SAVE

Saving money makes you feel good. Once you start to put some money aside, you will find:

- You can start planning to buy the things you really want.
- You can save up money for presents.
- You can keep some money in reserve to pay for unexpected expenses.

At least I've got enough money saved up to fix it.

STARTING SMALL

Even if you've very little money to spare, it's still possible to start saving. Just decide on the amount you think you could put aside each week or month, and try to stick to it. Be realistic about what you can save and don't give up. You'll find your savings soon start adding up.

A SAVINGS EXPERIMENT

At the end of each day, check your pockets or purse for any spare small coins and drop them into a jar — you'll probably find you don't miss them at all. Do this for a month, then count up what you've saved. You could use the money to buy something special or you could add it to your savings fund.

MAKE A SAVINGS PLAN

Whatever you're saving for, it helps to have a plan. First, set yourself a savings target (the total amount you need to save). Then you can work out how much you need to save each week, and how long it will take you to reach your target.

Once you've decided on your target, there are two ways to make a savings plan:

1) You can decide how much you want to save each week and calculate how long it will take to reach your target amount.

My savings target is £40. If I save £4 a week, it will take me 10 weeks to reach my target.

2) You can decide how long you want to save for and calculate how much you'll need to save each week.

I don't want to wait 10 weeks to save up £40, so I'm going to save £8 a week. Then I'll reach my target in 5 weeks.

Reaching a savings target feels very satisfying. And once you've reached one target, you can do it again and again.

I'm so glad I saved up for a guitar.

ADDING SAVINGS TO YOUR BUDGET

You can use your weekly budget* to help you plan your savings.

Joe has made a budget for the week showing his income and expenses:

Income		Expenses	
Allowance	£15.00	Lunch x 2	£8.00
Pet-sitting	£8.00	Bus tickets	£4.00
Total	£23.00	Total	£12.00

Once I've spent £12 on expenses, I'll have £11 left for other spending.

£23
- £12
= £11

Income	Expenses	Spending money
£23.00	£12.00	£11.00

* Turn back to page 36 to remind yourself about weekly budgets.

If I allow myself £6 for spending money, that will leave £5 for saving.

£11
- £6
= £5

Income	Expenses	Spending money	Savings
£23.00	£12.00	£6.00	£5.00

If I save £5 for the next 12 weeks, I will have saved £60. Then I'll have enough to buy the shoes I want.

£5
X 12
= £60

MONEY IN RESERVE

As well as saving up for something special, it's good to have some money in reserve. This is money you can use for emergencies — perhaps to repair a broken smartphone or to pay for a taxi if you've missed your bus.

Having money in reserve can also give you the freedom to act on impulse and spend some money on something just because it feels right.

When you're planning your budget, you can set aside some money each month for your reserve fund. Or you may simply choose to top up your reserve fund when it's running low.

BOOST YOUR SAVINGS

It's good to get into the habit of boosting your savings. If you have unspent money at the end of a week, consider adding it to your savings fund. And if you're given money as a present, you could put at least some of it into your savings.

TIME FOR A BANK ACCOUNT?

If you're thinking about long-term saving, you might want to consider a savings account. You'll find more about banks in Chapter 14.

Can you make a savings plan?

(Answers are on page 195.)

a) If you could afford to start saving £7 a week for buying presents, how much money would you have saved up for presents after 5 weeks?

b) Suppose you have 8 weeks to save for a wetsuit costing £80. If you save the same amount every week, how much should you set aside each week?

c) Imagine you have a plan to save £20 a month towards a bike costing £200. Luckily, you've been given £40 in birthday money. If you add your birthday money to your savings, how long will it take you to reach your savings target?

14

BANKS AND YOU

There are some very good reasons why people choose to open a bank account.

- Banks keep your money safe.
- They keep a record of how much money you have in your account, showing money coming in and money going out.
- If you save money with a bank, the bank will add interest payments to your savings. (See page 119.)

LOOKING AT BANK ACCOUNTS

Banks offer two basic types of account for over-18s — a current account and a savings account. Current accounts are used for managing everyday money, for example receiving wages and paying bills. Savings accounts help people to save by keeping their savings separate from their other money, and by adding a small amount of interest to their savings.

Banks also offer accounts for young customers.

- Youth bank accounts work like a regular current account but with added safety features to stop you spending money you don't have.
- Young saver accounts help you build up your savings. They may be used by the grown-ups in your life to save up money for you.

WHICH BANK?

Today, there are many types of bank to choose from. High street banks, building societies and digital-only banks all offer the same basic services, but with slightly different terms and conditions. This chapter gives information on different kinds of accounts, but choosing the right bank for you is a decision for you and your family to make.

YOUTH BANK ACCOUNTS

Youth bank accounts are designed for young
people who feel ready to start managing their own
money. As a youth bank account holder, you'll be
able to make deposits (put money into your
account) and make withdrawals (take money out
of your account).

What's the usual age range?

The usual age range for a youth bank account is
11 to 18. When you reach 18, the bank can transfer
your money to a regular current account.

Who can pay into my account?

Anyone can make a payment into a youth bank
account. So, if you have a part-time job, your
wages could be paid into your account.

Can I use online banking?

Most youth bank accounts offer online banking via
a computer, tablet or phone.

Do I get a bankcard?

All youth bank account holders are issued with a cash
card to take money out of their account. Some accounts
offer a debit card that can be used for spending, but
banks generally have to ask your parents' permission to
give you a debit card if you're under 16. (You can find
out more about bankcards on page 115.)

What makes a youth bank account different from an over-18 current account?

Youth account holders aren't allowed to have an overdraft. (You can read about overdrafts on page 148.) This means that if there's no money left in your account, your spending will be blocked automatically. This is a very important safety feature because it prevents you from getting into debt and facing heavy bank fees for borrowing money.

Some youth accounts have extra features. For example, you may want to have a monthly cap set on your spending. Once you've reached that limit, you won't be able to withdraw any money or use your card for spending. Having a capped account is a helpful way to limit your spending and stop you using up all your money at once.

MORE ABOUT BANKCARDS

When you open a youth bank account,
you will be issued with a bankcard and
a PIN (Personal Identification Number).

- You might have a **cash card** that allows you to take
  out cash from your account, using a cash machine.*
- You might have a **debit card** that allows you to take
  out cash AND spend money in shops and online.

KEEP YOUR PIN SAFE

Your PIN should be a secret that only you know.

Make sure you memorize it and never

share it with friends.

* Cash machines are sometimes called cashpoints or
  ATMs. ATM stands for Automated Teller Machine.

TAKING OUT CASH

Cash machines make taking out money simple and easy, but they need to be treated with care.

- Be careful when you're keying in your PIN. Always check that there's no one looking over your shoulder.
- Get into the habit of checking your balance (the amount of money in your account) before you draw out any cash.

DON'T PAY FOR YOUR CASH

Most cash machines are free to use, but some will charge you to withdraw your money. Look out for a sign saying FREE CASH WITHDRAWALS.

LOST CARD ALERT

If your card goes missing, you need to take action urgently. Phone your bank to CANCEL your card, or ask a parent or guardian to call for you. An operator will block all payments and cash withdrawals so someone else can't use your card, and will arrange for a replacement card to be sent to you.

PREPAID BANKCARDS

An easy way to avoid overspending is to use a prepaid bankcard, which you can get from your bank. With a prepaid card, you or your parents can decide exactly how much money you want to put on your card. Prepaid cards work like debit cards, allowing you to take out money and make payments. But when the money runs out, the card simply stops working until it's topped up again.

Prepaid cards are especially useful when you're travelling. It's much safer to carry a card than a wad of notes, and your parents may be able to top it up for you online in an emergency.

Help! I've run out of money!

YOUNG SAVER ACCOUNTS

With a young saver account, you can keep your savings in a safe place and watch them grow. Some young saver accounts run until the saver is 15, and some have an age limit of 17. At this stage, you can transfer your money to a regular savings account.

One advantage of keeping your savings in a bank is the interest the bank will pay you. Interest is a percentage of your total savings that is added to your savings each year. So, the larger your savings are, the more interest they will earn.

MORE ABOUT SAVINGS ACCOUNTS

Savings accounts are generally used for long-term saving, which means they may have conditions to prevent you taking out money whenever you want. For example, some young saver accounts require savers to give a set number of days' notice before withdrawing their money.

The percentage of interest added to your savings each year is shown as an AER, or Annual Equivalent Rate. This rate is used as a way of comparing different savings schemes. The higher the AER, the more interest you will gain on your savings.

Interest rates on savings are much smaller than the interest rates that people are charged when they're paying back a loan. (These rates are known as APR and you can read about them on page 150.) This means you will only see a serious benefit if your savings are large (say over £1,000). Young saver accounts are often used by adults to deposit money for a child to use when they are older.

ONLINE BANKING

Many people nowadays manage
their bank account online. With
an online account, you can:

- Access your bank account from
  a computer, tablet or smartphone.
- Check your bank balance any time you want.
- See exactly what's been paid in and what's
  gone out.
- Make payments to another person simply by
  typing the details of their bank account.
- Pay bills and set up regular payments.
  (See Chapter 17 for more on paying bills.)

SPECIAL FEATURES

Some online bank accounts are specially designed to make banking easier for young people. They work on smartphones and tablets and include such features as:

- Alerts to warn you when you're in danger of running out of money.
- Programs to help you save a certain amount each week.
- Systems to record your purchases in different categories, so you can review your spending patterns.

I find it really helpful to receive text alerts when my account is getting low.

ONLINE BANKING SAFETY

When you bank online, you need to take special care.

- Keep your login information strictly secret.
- Don't use the same password for your online banking as you do for other websites.
- Never use free Wi-Fi in cafés or shops to log in to your bank account, because other users may be able to access your personal details.

WATCH OUT FOR FRAUD

Some criminals try to gain access to bank accounts by sending a message by text, phone or email. These messages appear to be from your bank and may request login details for your account, or ask you to type in your password. Don't reply. Ask a grown-up to check any message that seems suspicious and never give login details by phone or email.

15

WORK AND PAY

In the future, you'll find yourself facing all sorts of exciting new challenges. You may be starting a full-time job, beginning an apprenticeship, or studying at college or university, and all of these options will bring new money choices. This chapter covers work and pay, and the following chapter gives advice on student finance.

WHAT'S AN APPRENTICESHIP?

Apprentices combine work and study by mixing on-the-job training with classroom learning, either at a college or training centre. They are paid either wages or a salary and have time off for study (usually one day a week). An apprenticeship usually lasts between one and five years.

STARTING FULL-TIME WORK

Once you start full-time work, you will receive regular pay.

- **You may be paid wages.**

Wages are payment for the hours you work, using a set hourly rate. They're usually paid monthly, but some employers pay weekly or daily wages.

- **You may get a salary.**

Employees on a salary receive a monthly payment in return for working a certain number of hours a week. Salaries are paid directly into an employee's bank account.

> Not everyone is paid wages or a salary. You can see some other kinds of payment on page 129.

WHAT'S THE MINIMUM WAGE?

In many countries, the government sets a minimum rate of pay per hour, and it is illegal for employers to pay under that sum. In the UK, the minimum wage applies to all workers over 25 and there are also junior rates and rates for apprentices.

LOOKING AT SALARIES

Salaries are shown as the amount you earn each year. But this isn't the same as the pay you take home. A salary is the amount you earn before income tax and other charges are taken off.

Turn to page 130 to find out more about pay.

My annual salary is £20,000, but my take home pay is £16,980 a year and I'm paid £1,415 a month.

HOW MANY HOURS?

In the UK, the usual number of working hours for a full-time worker is between 30 and 40 a week. However, some workers, such as doctors, are expected to work for many more hours than this. The number of hours you're expected to work is stated in your contract of employment.

WHAT'S A ZERO-HOURS CONTRACT?

Most employment contracts guarantee that the employee will be given work for a certain number of hours each week. But zero-hours contracts don't make this promise. This means that some weeks there may be no work at all. Workers on a zero-hours contract can face difficult challenges with their financial planning.

WHAT ABOUT OVERTIME?

When you do overtime, you work for longer than the hours agreed in your contract. Overtime work is often paid at a higher rate than usual. A worker may also be given extra pay for working 'anti-social hours', such as during a public holiday.

Some employees aren't paid extra for overtime. Instead, they can take time off to make up for any overtime hours that they've worked. This is sometimes known as time off in lieu (TOIL).

ALL KINDS OF WORK

People can be paid for their work in a range
of ways. Here are some examples:

I'm a freelance designer. I charge
an hourly rate for my work.

 I run my own business. I pay myself a
salary from the profits of my business,
and I pay my employees' salaries too.

I'm a picture framer. I have a set
of prices that I charge my customers.

 I sell cars. As well as my salary,
I earn extra payment, known as
commission, on every car I sell.

LOOKING AT PAY

Your pay isn't simply the money you've earned. It also includes deductions — money **taken off** your earnings by the government and other organizations.

Looking at a payslip, you will see:

- Your gross monthly pay
  This is your pay <u>before</u> any deductions.
- Your net monthly pay
  This is your pay <u>after</u> deductions.
- Your income tax payment
- Your National Insurance payment
  These are payments all workers have to make to the government.

You may also see:

- A student loan repayment
  See Chapter 16.
- A workplace pension contribution
  Turn to page 132 to find out more.

WHAT IS INCOME TAX?

Income tax is a proportion of people's earnings that goes to the government to pay for public services, such as hospitals, schools and the police.

Tax payments don't start until a worker is earning a certain amount, which is set by the government each year.

Because income tax is a proportion of what you earn, people earning a large amount of money pay more tax than people with smaller incomes.

WHAT IS NATIONAL INSURANCE?

National Insurance is the name for a system of payments that are taken off people's earnings and given to the government. They go into a fund that helps to pay for state benefits, such as maternity leave and the state pension.

PAYING FOR A PENSION

Saving up for retirement doesn't seem remotely urgent when you're young, but it makes very good sense to start saving early. If you put it off until later, you'll need to make much larger payments just to save the same amount.

Full-time workers in the UK are encouraged to save for a pension, once they've passed a certain earnings threshold. If you're 22 or over and you earn more than £10,000 a year, you will be required to pay a contribution into a workplace pension fund. Unless you make the decision to opt out, this contribution will be taken off your pay automatically.

Workplace pension funds are a great way to boost your retirement savings because your employer has to add a contribution each month.

This is the life!

STUDENT FINANCE

16

If you decide to go to college or university in the UK, you can apply for a loan from the Student Loans Company (SLC). The SLC is a government-funded organization that pays for higher education. You pay the money back to the SLC when you're earning enough to afford repayments.

- **Most students apply for a tuition fee loan.** This covers the basic costs of a university course. Tuition fees are paid directly to the college or university.

- **Many also take out a maintenance costs loan.** This helps to cover everyday living costs, such as accommodation, food and transport. Maintenance money is paid directly to the student. The amount a student can borrow depends on how much their parents earn.

MANAGING A MAINTENANCE LOAN

Maintenance loans are usually split into three payments over the course of a year. These are paid directly into your bank account so it's up to you to use your budgeting skills to make sure you have the funds for the things you really need.

PAYING BACK A STUDENT LOAN

Paying back a student loan is very different from paying back other loans. (You can read about loans in Chapter 19.)

- You don't have to start repaying your loan until you've started earning over a certain amount. (Currently, the threshold for repayments is a salary of £25,000 a year.)

- After you reach the repayment threshold, you have to pay a percentage of any money you earn over that threshold. The current repayment rate is 9%. So, if you earn £30,000 a year, you will pay 9% of £5,000 (the amount you've earned above the threshold). This amounts to £450 a year.

- Once you start repaying your loan, the repayments are taken out of your salary automatically.

- After 30 years, any unpaid money you owe is cancelled. So, if you haven't earned enough to pay back all the loan, or if you haven't even started to pay it off, you won't be left with a debt forever.

I earn enough in my new job to start paying back my student loan.

BURSARIES, GRANTS AND SCHOLARSHIPS

There are a few extra sources of finance that can help some students cover their expenses. (Find out more on Usborne Quicklinks, see page 4.)

- Many universities offer bursaries to students from low income households. These are usually one-off sums of money (for example £1,000) and they do not need to be repaid.

- Some universities and companies offer scholarships to promising students. This money is often used to pay the tuition fees for a course.

- Some universities offer grants for a specific purpose, such as a study trip abroad.

STAR ACADEMY

PART-TIME JOBS

Some students take on part-time work or find a job in the holidays. These extra earnings can help to cover the cost of student life, but combining study with work can be a challenge.

STUDENT DISCOUNTS

Once you have a student card, you can get discounts in shops, restaurants, cinemas and gyms. There are also some really good travel deals for young people. It's tempting to take advantage of discounts, but you'll need to be careful to not get carried away.

17. PAYING BILLS

As you get older, you'll find you have lots of bills to pay. As well as household bills for services such as electricity, gas and water, there may be phone bills, regular insurance or subscription payments — and more.

So, how do you stay on top of your bills and make sure they all get paid on time? The most important thing is to get organized...

TOP TIPS
FOR MANAGING BILLS

- As soon as you get a bill, check it carefully.
  If you spot a problem early, you'll have more
  time to sort it out before it's time to pay up.

- Note the 'payment due' date and give yourself
  a reminder to pay well in advance.
  Highlight payment dates in your diary
  or set alerts on your phone.

- Store your bills in a safe place.
  If your bills are digital, you could set up
  a folder on your computer.

- Set up a payment system that works for you.
  Many people choose to pay their bills by direct
  debit. Turn over the page to find out more.

PAYING BY DIRECT DEBIT

Once you are over 18, you can set up a direct debit arrangement with your bank. This allows a company or an organization to take money out of your bank account on agreed dates. Once you've set up a direct debit, money is taken automatically from your bank account on the date your bill is due.

If you pay by direct debit, you'll never miss a payment and you'll never be late with your payments. But you will need to keep a careful check on your bank account to see what money has been taken out and when.

ELECTRICITY

MAGAZINE SUBSCRIPTION

WATER

INSURANCE

Phone

DIRECT DEBIT OR STANDING ORDER?

Direct debits and standing orders are both methods of making automatic payments from a bank account, but they work in different ways and are used for different kinds of payment.

- For a **direct debit**, the amount leaving your account is decided by the company you're paying. So, the amount might change from month to month depending on the size of your bill. Direct debits are used for paying monthly bills, or rent payments.

- For a **standing order**, the amount leaving your account is decided by you, and the amount won't change unless you give instructions. Standing orders are used for regular payments that don't usually change, such as annual subscriptions or donations to charity.

18

RENTING AND MORTGAGES

Sometime in the future, you may start making plans to move into a rented flat or house. And looking further ahead, you may even dream of buying a home of your own. This chapter covers some of the costs involved in renting and taking out a mortgage. It also provides a guide to the regular costs of running a home.

GETTING READY TO RENT

Moving into a house or flat is an exciting step, but it comes with costs. Before you move in:

- You will be asked to pay your first month's rent in advance.
- You'll probably be asked to pay a tenancy deposit (see page 144).
- You may need to pay a letting agent's fee.
- If the place is unfurnished, you will need to buy furniture.

We need some chairs!

WHAT IS A TENANCY DEPOSIT?

A tenancy deposit is a sum of money paid as a guarantee to cover the cost of possible damage to a rented property. The cost of a tenancy deposit is usually about the same as one month's rent, and is kept until the tenants move out. It is returned in full if the landlord is satisfied that there is no damage.

BUYING YOUR OWN HOME

It's a wonderful dream to own your own home, but how do you go about it? Unless you're extremely wealthy, you'll need to take out a mortgage.

WHAT IS A MORTGAGE?

Most home-buyers have a repayment mortgage. This is a long-term loan from a bank or building society that allows people to buy a house or a flat. The home-buyers repay the loan in monthly instalments, with added interest payments (see page 149). Paying back a mortgage usually takes at least 25 years.

PAYING A MORTGAGE DEPOSIT

The first step towards taking out a mortgage is to save up for a deposit. This is a chunk of money that provides the first payment on a property. In the UK, a mortgage deposit is usually between five and twenty per cent of the property's total cost.

A LONG-TERM INVESTMENT

Because mortgage payments include added interest, home-buyers end up paying a lot more for their home than its original selling price. However, most people think having a mortgage is a good idea. If you take out a mortgage instead of renting, your payments are helping to pay for your own home, rather than going into your landlord's bank.

HOUSEHOLD EXPENSES

Once you are living in a place of your own, you'll need to think about your regular household expenses. These are some of the costs you'll need to budget for:

- Monthly rent or mortgage payments.
- Bills for gas, electricity and water (unless they're included in your rent).
- Broadband line rental.
- Council tax payments (unless included in the rent). These are payments for local services, such as rubbish collection.

It's a good idea to set up a household budget showing all your costs for the month. This will help you plan your spending to make sure you can always pay the rent and the bills.

BORROWING MONEY

19

Most people borrow money at some time in their lives.

- A student may have an arranged overdraft to cover unexpected costs.
- A family may have a credit card that they use for booking holidays.
- Someone who is self-employed may take out a bank loan to help buy tools or a vehicle.

Borrowing money can be very useful in helping people to achieve their goals. But borrowers need to manage their loans carefully, to make sure they can pay back what they owe.

This chapter looks at different kinds of borrowing and the risks that they can bring with them.

LOOKING AT OVERDRAFTS

Once you have an over-18 current account, you may
be able to have an arranged overdraft. This will allow
you to withdraw extra money from your account up
to an agreed limit. Some bank accounts (such as
student accounts) offer arranged overdrafts that
are interest-free, but most account holders are
charged interest for using money from an overdraft.

WHAT ABOUT UNARRANGED OVERDRAFTS?

Going overdrawn without authorisation from your
bank is NEVER a good idea. Charges for using an
unarranged overdraft can be as high as £20 a week.

If the money in a current account is getting low, it's
easy to go overdrawn without realizing it. Once you
have an over-18 current account, you'll need to keep
a close watch on your balance to
make sure you never
go overdrawn.

You owe the
bank £40.

ADDING INTEREST

Have you ever borrowed money from someone you know? If so, you may have promised to pay it back within a certain time, but you probably didn't have to pay any extra charges.

Sadly, the world of loans doesn't work like this. When you borrow money from a bank or company, you agree to pay back the loan AND to pay interest on the amount you've borrowed. Interest is a percentage of the total sum you've borrowed and it can range in size enormously.

Oh no! I have to pay back my loan and pay the interest payments too!

LOOKING AT INTEREST RATES

The amount of interest you pay on a loan is shown as an APR, or Annual Percentage Rate. All lenders are required by law to show their APR, and this helps borrowers to compare interest rates. Credit cards have a much higher APR than bank loans and the APR on store cards is even higher than on credit cards.

MAKING REPAYMENTS

Most repayments on loans are made in monthly instalments with interest added to each payment you make. So, the longer you take to repay the loan, the more interest payments you will have to make, and the more money you'll end up paying.

TYPES OF BORROWING

There are many different ways to borrow, but here are just a few.

• Bank loans

Banks offer loans to their customers, so long as they are sure that the borrower can afford the repayments. Banks charge lower interest rates on repayments than most other lenders.

• Hire purchase deals

Some sellers of expensive items, such as cars or furniture, allow their customers to pay in monthly instalments plus interest. Customers can take away their purchase straightaway, but paying back the loan can take months or years and end up costing a lot more than the original price.

It took me five years to buy my car and cost me £5,000 more than its original price.

- Credit cards

Credit card companies allow card users to borrow money up to an agreed limit. Card holders use their cards for spending and pay back what they've borrowed in monthly instalments.

CREDIT CARD REPAYMENTS

Credit card companies offer three monthly repayment options:

- You can pay back the full amount you owe.
- You can pay back part of what you owe.
- You can make the minimum payment.

If you repay the full amount, you will only have to pay a small handling charge, but if you choose one of the other options, you will have to pay interest and it will keep mounting up each month.

CREDIT CARD DANGER £££

If you just make the minimum repayment each month, your repayments could drag on for years, with the amount that you have to pay back growing every month. A borrower could spend 30 years paying off a debt of £3,000, and end up paying many times the original debt because of all the interest that has mounted up.

• Store cards

Store cards can be used for shopping in a store or a chain of stores. They have lots of tempting special offers, but they have extremely high interest rates.

I thought my store card would save me money, but it's cost me a fortune!

CHANGING RATES

Some loans have a fixed interest rate, so borrowers know exactly how much interest they'll be paying each month, but many loans have a variable rate. This means borrowers need to keep checking to see how much interest they'll be paying.

Credit card and store card companies often offer a low interest rate as a way of encouraging people to borrow. But once a borrower starts using their card, interest rates can rise very sharply. Card holders should always check the APR on their monthly statement. If they are unhappy about the interest rate, they have the right to change to a different card.

I never imagined interest rates could rise so steeply.

PROBLEMS WITH REPAYMENTS

Borrowers who are late with their repayments on a loan or a card have to pay a fine. And if they miss a payment or their payment is very late, it will affect their credit score.

WHAT'S A CREDIT SCORE?

A credit score is a record of a borrower's repayments on loans and cards. When people apply to a lender for a loan or a mortgage, the lender checks their credit score before deciding whether or not to offer them the loan. (Credit scores are sometimes known as credit ratings.)

EMERGENCY BORROWING

People in financial difficulty may sometimes need a short-term loan just to keep them going until their next payday or until they can get hold of some more money. 'Payday' loan companies offer short-term loans, but they charge their borrowers very high repayment rates.

BEWARE OF LOAN SHARKS

Sometimes, people in need of money may turn to illegal lenders — often known as 'loan sharks'. These lenders may start off seeming friendly, but if a borrower falls behind with repayments, they can soon turn very nasty. Instead of sticking to a set interest rate, they raise their repayment rates whenever they wish, and may even use violence to get the money they want.

GETTING INTO DEBT

Once repayments start mounting up, people can find themselves struggling to pay back what they owe. It's all too easy to get caught in a vicious circle, where borrowers need to borrow more in order to make their repayments.

Trying to keep up with loan repayments can feel like running as fast as you can, but still falling behind.

Fortunately, there are places where people can go to discuss their debt problems and get help with managing repayments. Go to Usborne Quicklinks (see page 4) for links to helpful websites.

FOUR GOLDEN RULES OF BORROWING

DON'T BORROW MORE THAN YOU HAVE TO

The bigger the loan you take out, the bigger the repayments will be.

PAY THE MONEY BACK AS SOON AS YOU CAN

The longer you take to repay a loan, the more the costs will mount up.

MAKE SURE YOU HAVE A PLAN FOR REPAYING YOUR LOAN

Set aside enough money each month to make the repayments.

BE SURE NOT TO MISS A REPAYMENT

Missing a repayment will mean you have to pay extra fees and can affect your credit score (see page 155).

GAMBLING

20

When people gamble, they take risks with their money, even though they know that the chance of losing is much greater than the chance of winning.

Gambling can happen in a public place, such as a casino, a games arcade or a betting shop. People can gamble at home and can access betting sites on the internet. Internet gambling is a very big business and many people gamble online in secret. Gambling is a high-risk activity, and for some people it can be dangerously addictive.

GAMBLING CAN START EARLY

It is against the law to gamble if
you're under 18, but there is evidence
that gambling can start early. Some under-18s bet
on card games and play on slot machines. Children are
widely exposed to gambling ads, and many computer
games mimic the experience of gambling as players
compete to build up piles of virtual money.

GAMBLING IS ADDICTIVE

Some people find that once they start gambling,
they just can't stop. Even though they know
they're losing money, they keep on going, in
the hope that their luck will change. Gamblers
can easily get caught in a trap, where the more
they lose, the more desperate they
become to win their money back.

INVESTING

21

Some people decide to use a portion of their money for investing. This involves putting money into something that you believe will grow in value. Investments can bring rewards, but they can also be risky, and investors can lose the money they invested. Before investing money, people need to ask themselves:

- How much money can I afford to lose?
- Do I really need this money for something else?

DIFFERENT INVESTMENTS

People can choose to invest in a range of things. Some investors buy property and some buy art or classic cars, but the most common form of investment is to buy shares in a company or other organization.

BUYING SHARES

When investors buy shares in a company, they provide part of the money that's used to run that company. Companies are funded by millions of shares, so each share is a tiny part of the company's total wealth.

WHAT HAPPENS TO SHARES?

Shares can go up or down in value, depending on the success of the company.

- If a company does well, the value of its shares will rise. So, if investors sell their shares, they will make a profit.

↑ **PROFIT**

LOSS ↓

- If a company doesn't do as well as expected, the value of its shares will fall. So, if investors sell their shares, they will make a loss.

I bought 100 shares at £1 a share. The company has grown fast and now my shares are worth £3 each.

IF YOU SELL YOUR 100 SHARES NOW, YOU WILL BE PAID £300, AND MAKE A PROFIT OF £200 ON YOUR INVESTMENT.

I also bought 100 shares at £1 a share. The company hasn't done well and now my shares are worth 20p each.

IF YOU SELL YOUR 100 SHARES NOW, YOU WILL BE PAID £20, AND MAKE A LOSS OF £80 ON YOUR INVESTMENT.

PAYING DIVIDENDS

As well as making money from selling shares, shareholders may receive dividend payments from the company they've invested in. A dividend is a small share of a company's profit that is paid out to its shareholders. The size of the dividend depends on how successful the company has been in a year and how many shares a shareholder owns.

INVESTMENT CHOICES

Before people make the decision to invest their money, they need to ask themselves:

- How much can I afford to invest?
- How long can I manage without the money I've invested?
- Do I want to go for a high-risk investment, which could earn more money, but could also lose everything I've put in?
- Do I prefer a lower-risk investment, which probably won't make so much money, but is more likely to keep my money safe?

The world of investment is very complicated, so people often rely on experts to help them make their investment choices. Financial experts advise their clients on which companies to invest in, and on the best times to buy and sell shares.

22. INSURANCE

Sometimes, unexpected things can ruin your financial plans. You may damage your phone, lose your wallet or crash your bike. And, further in the future, you may face a range of expensive problems. Imagine how you'd feel if your car broke down or your home was flooded, or if you had an accident and lost your job. Serious problems like these are hard enough to deal with on their own, without the added worry of finding the money to pay for them.

So, how do you take steps to protect your money and make sure that, if you have a problem, it doesn't end up costing you a fortune?

BE PREPARED

People can prepare themselves for unexpected costs in these ways:

- Keeping money in reserve for emergencies
  Turn back to page 106 for advice on saving up money to keep in reserve.
- Taking out insurance
  Read the rest of this chapter to find out more.

WHAT IS INSURANCE?

Insurance is a way to protect yourself from paying out lots of money if things go wrong. People make regular payments (either once a year or once a month) to an insurance company in return for an insurance policy. The policy provides a guarantee to pay most of the costs if certain problems occur. As soon as people start paying for their policy, they are protected and they have the right to claim money from their insurance company.

ALL KINDS OF INSURANCE

You can take out insurance on your home, your possessions or your car and many other aspects of your life. (Turn to page 174 to find out more.)

Some insurance policies are compulsory. It's against the law to drive a vehicle that is uninsured, and you can't take out a mortgage on a property unless you have home buildings insurance. For other policies, people have to make their own decisions about whether they need protection or not.

GET PROTECTED

Even though some insurance isn't compulsory, you could be taking a risk if you don't protect yourself. If you were going abroad, it would be a serious mistake to try to cut your costs by not paying for travel insurance.

HOW DOES INSURANCE WORK?

When people take out an insurance policy, they make a payment, called a premium, which can be paid monthly or yearly. The cost of the premium depends on the size of the risk and the value of what's being insured.

I'm an inexperienced driver so my motor insurance premium is high.

I've been driving for 20 years without any accidents so my premium is much lower than yours.

I drive a very expensive car so my premium is high.

My car would cost much less to repair than yours, so my premium is lower.

MAKING INSURANCE CLAIMS

When a problem occurs, policyholders fill in a claim form. The details of the claim are checked carefully before the insurance company agrees to pay out money.

Policyholders with a history of making lots of claims have to pay more for their insurance than people with fewer claims. People who haven't made any claims over a certain number of years are rewarded by having money taken off the cost of their policy. This is called a 'no claims bonus'.

OH NO! There goes my no claims bonus!

CLUNK!

CRUNCH!

MOTOR INSURANCE

If you own a vehicle, you have to buy motor insurance to help cover the cost of accidents and other problems. There are three types of insurance to choose between:

- Third party
  Covers the cost of damage to another person's vehicle or property.
- Third party, fire and theft
  Covers the same costs as third party insurance, with added financial cover if your vehicle is stolen or damaged by fire.
- Fully comprehensive
  Covers all the costs described above, plus the cost of damage to your own vehicle.

The fully comprehensive policy is the most expensive, but if you choose one of the cheaper options, you risk facing some very large costs if something goes wrong.

HOME BUILDINGS INSURANCE

All mortgage payers have to take out a home buildings insurance policy. This covers the cost of repairing a property if it is damaged in some way, for example, in a fire or a storm.

HOME CONTENTS INSURANCE

Home contents insurance covers the cost of replacing possessions that have been accidentally damaged or stolen. Clothes, computers, bicycles and mobile phones can all be included in a home contents insurance policy, even if they are lost or damaged outside the home.

TRAVEL INSURANCE

Travel insurance covers a range of expenses that travellers may face when they go on holiday or travel for work.

Most travel policies cover the cost of:

- Replacing lost or stolen bags and their contents.
- Expenses if flights are delayed or there are other travel problems.
- Having to cancel or cut short a holiday.
- Emergency medical expenses. (Travellers have to pay more for their insurance if they're going on a high-risk holiday, such as a climbing or snowboarding trip.)

OTHER INSURANCE TYPES

It's possible to insure many different things,
but here are some of the most common policies:

- Health insurance
  Covers some of the costs of medical
  treatment or care.
- Income protection
  Guarantees some income if the policyholder
  is unable to work.
- Loan protection
  Covers the costs of repaying a loan, if the
  borrower becomes unemployed.
- Life insurance
  Pays out money to family or other dependents
  if the policyholder dies.
- Pet insurance
  Covers the costs
  of vets' bills.

FINDING HELP AND ADVICE

Now that you've read this book, you should be
feeling confident about managing your money, but
there may be times when you could do with advice.

If you're having problems, it's good to talk to
someone you know well. There are also some
useful websites offering clear advice on money
management. Some of these sites have online
helplines with trained advisors who can give
personal support and advice. You'll find links
to websites on Usborne Quicklinks, see page 4.

MONEY WORDS AND TERMS

AER — AER stands for Annual Equivalent Rate. AER is used as a way of comparing different interest rates on savings.

allowance — regular money paid by parents or guardians to their children.

app — a software application that is designed to perform special functions and can be downloaded onto a phone, tablet or other computer device.

APR — APR stands for Annual Percentage Rate. APR is used as a way of comparing different interest rates on loan repayments.

arranged overdraft — see **overdraft**.

ATM — see **cash machine**.

bank account — a service offered by a bank or building society, allowing you to pay in money, take out cash and pay bills etc. The bank keeps a record of everything that happens to your money.

bank balance — the amount of money you have in your bank account.

bankcard — a plastic card issued by your bank or building society that gives you access to the money in your bank account. Bankcards may be cash cards or debit cards.

bank loan — money that bank account holders arrange to borrow from their bank and then pay back, with an interest rate that has been arranged in advance.

benefits — payments made by the government to certain groups of people. Disability benefit, child benefit and maternity benefit are all examples of benefits paid for by the state.

budget — a way of planning your finances, in which you set out your income and expenses, then plan how to spend the rest of your money.

building society — an organization that is owned by its members, who have shares in the society. Building societies offer the same services as banks.

cash machine — a machine that allows people to use their bankcards to take out cash and check their bank balance. Other names for a cash machine are cashpoint, hole-in-the-wall, and ATM. ATM stands for Automated Teller Machine.

contactless payment — a way of making a payment by waving or tapping a contactless device (such as a bankcard or a phone) on or near a contactless reader.

contract — a legal agreement between one person or organization and another person or organization, that says what both sides must do. For example, you could have a contract with an employer, or with a phone company.

council tax — money paid by homeowners and renters to their local council to pay for local services, such as street lighting and rubbish collection.

credit — money put into an account is 'credited' to that account. If an account is 'in credit', there is money in it that is available to spend. Another term for being in credit, is 'being in the black'.

credit card — a plastic card available to over 18 year-olds that allows you to borrow money in order to make purchases. Credit cards have very high rates of interest on their repayments.

credit note — see **credit voucher.**

credit score — a score given by a credit agency based on your history of borrowing and repayments. Your credit score reflects the level of risk involved in lending money to you. Another name for credit score is 'credit rating'.

credit voucher — a card or note issued by a store when a purchase is returned, allowing the customer to make an alternative purchase.

cryptocurrency — virtual money that can be used online to buy and sell products and services.

currency — money used in a particular country, for example, pounds, dollars and yen.

current account — a bank account that is used to manage day-to-day money, for example, receiving wages and paying bills.

data — mobile data allows mobile devices such as smartphones and tablets to access the internet when a Wi-Fi connection isn't available.

debit — money taken out of an account is 'debited' to that account. If an account is 'in debit', there is money owed on the account. Another term for being in debit, is 'being in the red'.

debit card — a bankcard used to pay for things online or in a shop without using cash. You can also use a debit card to withdraw money from your bank account, using a cash machine.

debt — money you owe to another person or organization.

deduction — money taken off a salary for income tax or other payments.

deposit — money paid into a bank account. See also **tenancy deposit** and **mortgage deposit.**

direct debit — an instruction to a bank to release money from an account to make regular payments automatically. The billing company makes a direct request to the bank and can often change the amount requested.

discount — money taken off the price of something.

dividend — money from a company's profits paid to people who have shares in the company.

employee — someone who is paid to work for an organization, company or individual.

employer — an organization, company or individual who pays somebody else to work for them.

expenses — things you spend money on in order to live. Food and rent are examples of expenses.

Fairtrade — the Fairtrade movement aims to make sure that producers and workers are paid fairly for their work.

fixed interest rate — an interest rate that is guaranteed to stay the same for a fixed period of time.

fraud — the crime of deceiving people in some way, often to gain money.

gambling — risking money on a game or other activity at which you can win or lose.

gross income — the total pay that people receive before any deductions (such as income tax) are made.

hire purchase — a way of paying for goods by borrowing the total cost and making regular repayments. Hire purchase is sometimes known as HP.

in-app purchase — a purchase made inside an app.

income — money that you earn or receive. Your income is your 'money in'.

income protection — see **insurance**.

income tax — a tax that has to be paid on the money people earn, once their earnings reach a certain level.

insurance — a way to protect yourself from losing money if something goes wrong. You make a regular payment (known as a premium) to an insurance company in return for their guarantee of some financial protection. There are many different types of insurance such as motor insurance, home contents and home buildings insurance, travel insurance and life insurance.

interest — money that is added to loan repayments or to savings in a bank account.

interest rate — a set percentage of a loan or of savings that determines how much interest is paid.

investing — using money to buy something that may increase in value over time, for example shares in a company.

letting agent — someone who helps a landlord to find tenants and organizes rent payments and repairs.

loan — a sum of money that you borrow from a bank, an organization or an individual, usually with interest added.

loan shark — someone who lends money without following the laws on lending.

maintenance loan — a loan available to students to cover day-to-day living costs.

minimum repayment — the smallest possible amount that must be paid off each month on a credit card or store card debt.

minimum wage — the lowest hourly wage that employers are allowed to pay by law.

mortgage — a long-term loan from a building society or bank that allows people to buy their own home. Mortgages are paid back over a number of years.

mortgage deposit — a sum of money that people must pay upfront towards the cost of a property when they are taking out a mortgage to buy it.

National Insurance — money taken off people's earnings to pay for benefits, such as state pensions.

needs — things you cannot do without.

net income — the pay that people receive after deductions, such as income tax, are made. Net income is sometimes called take-home pay.

online banking — a method of managing your bank account from your phone, tablet or computer.

overdraft — a way of borrowing money from your bank through your current account. An arranged overdraft will allow you to spend money up to an agreed amount. If an overdraft is unauthorised, the borrower will have to pay heavy fees.

overtime — time worked in addition to the hours agreed in a contract of employment. Overtime can be paid or unpaid.

payday lender — a lender who provides a short-term loan but charges extremely high rates of interest on the loan.

pension — regular payments made to people who have reached retirement age. There are three basic kinds of pension: a state pension, paid by the government; a private pension, paid by a private pension company; and a workplace pension. See **workplace pension**.

PIN — PIN stands for Personal Identification Number. This is a four-digit security number that is used with credit cards, bankcards and online banking.

prepaid bankcard — a bankcard with money paid onto it in advance. Prepaid cards can be used for spending and withdrawing money.

profit — the amount of money left over after subtracting all costs and expenses.

receipt — a document given by a seller to a buyer as proof of a purchase. Receipts may be in paper or electronic form.

rent — money paid by a tenant to the owner of a property (such as a house or a flat).

salary — a regular payment made by an employer to an employee. Salaries are usually paid once a month directly into an employee's bank account.

savings account — a bank account designed for saving money. The bank pays you interest on your savings.

shares — tiny parts of a company that are paid for by investors, known as shareholders.

smartphone — a touch-screen phone that can access the internet.

standing order — an instruction to a bank to release money from an account to make payments automatically. Only the account holder can change the payments.

statement — a document that shows all your recent financial activity.

store card — a card issued by a shop or a chain of shops that works like a credit card. Store cards have even higher interest rates on repayments than credit cards.

store credits — see **credit voucher.**

student loan — see **maintenance loan** and **tuition fee loan.**

Student Loans Company — an organization that provides loans to students in universities and colleges in the UK to pay for their tuition and maintenance. The Student Loans Company is often known as the SLC and is owned by the British Government.

subscription — a regular payment for a product, such as a mobile app or a magazine, or for a service such as membership of a club. Subscriptions are often paid monthly.

tablet — a small, portable computer with a touch screen.

tariff — a fixed number of call-minutes, texts and data set out in a phone contract.

tax — money paid to the government. There are various taxes, including income tax, vehicle tax and value added tax (VAT). VAT is paid on some goods and services.

tax allowance — the amount of money you can earn before you need to pay income tax.

tenancy deposit — money paid by a tenant before moving into a rented property as a way of protecting a landlord from the cost of any damage caused by that tenant.

tenant — someone who lives in a property rented from a landlord.

tuition fee loan — a loan that covers the cost of a university or college course.

unarranged overdraft — borrowing money from a bank without asking permission in advance. If you have an unarranged overdraft, you can face very large charges.

unit price — the price for one item or measurement (such as one kilogram or one litre), that can be used to compare the same type of goods sold in varying packages.

variable interest rate — an interest rate on repayments that is not fixed, so the size of the interest payments can change.

wages — the amount someone is paid for a job. Wages are usually paid monthly or weekly.

wants — things you would like to buy, but you could do without. See also **needs**.

Wi-Fi — a wireless connection to an internet router, which provides internet to homes and businesses. Wi-Fi connections are only available close to the router.

withdrawal — money taken out of a bank or building society account.

workplace pension — a pension set up by employers for their employees. A percentage of an employee's salary is paid into a pension fund and the employer also contributes to each employee's pension.

zero-hours contract — a contract of employment that does not guarantee a minimum number of hours' work.

QUIZ ANSWERS

page 30

<u>Wants</u>: bubblegum, cinema ticket, lipstick,
magazine, perfume, sweets.

<u>Needs</u>: banana, bus ticket, deodorant, sandwiches,
socks, toothpaste.

page 52

a) Materials cost per puppet = £2.50

b) Labour cost per puppet = £2

c) Total cost per puppet = £4.50

d) You should charge £6 for each puppet.

page 67

The best deals are:

a) 2 for 1, c) 2/3 original price, f) 60% off

The new discounted prices are: Shorts: £15, T-shirt: £8

page 108

a) You would have £35 to spend on presents.

b) You should set aside £10 each week.

c) You will reach your savings target in 8 months.

INDEX

A

B

I

J

L

M

N

O

R

S

T

Additional editing by
Jessica Greenwell and Hannah Watson

With additional design by Tilly Kitching

Usborne Publishing Ltd., Usborne House, 83-85 Saffron Hill,
London EC1N 8RT, England. www.usborne.com Printed in the UK.
First published in 2019. Copyright © 2019 Usborne Publishing Ltd. UKE.

When using the internet, please follow the internet safety guidelines shown
at the Usborne Quicklinks website. The links at Usborne Quicklinks are
regularly reviewed and updated, but Usborne Publishing is not repsonsible and
does not accept liability for the content of any website other than its own.
We recommend that all children are supervised while using the internet.